Brave and Beautiful Queen Esther

Written by Jennifer Holder
Illustrated by Terry Julien

Based on Esther 2–8

Brave and Beautiful Queen Esther copyright © 2009 by Tyndale House Publishers, Inc., Carol Stream, IL 60188. All rights reserved. www.tyndale.com. Originally published as a Happy Day book by Standard Publishing, Cincinnati, Ohio. First printing by Tyndale House Publishers, Inc., in 2015. Cover design: Andrew Quach. *TYNDALE*, Tyndale's quill logo, and *Faith That Sticks* are registered trademarks of Tyndale House Publishers, Inc. For manufacturing information regarding this product, please call 1-800-323-9400.

ISBN 978-1-4964-0314-8

Printed in China

| 21 | 20 | 19 | 18 | 17 | 16 | 1! |
| 7 | 6 | 5 | 4 | 3 | 2 | 1 |

D1275147

Tyndale House Publishers, Inc.
Carol Stream, Illinois

Long ago there lived a young girl named Esther. Esther was raised by her older cousin, Mordecai, because both of her parents had died. As Esther grew up, she became more and more beautiful.

A time came when the king of the land was looking for a wife. Of all the girls in his kingdom, the king was most pleased with Esther. So she became queen.

Throughout history, queens have chosen the loveliest clothes, found the best beauty treatments, and, most importantly, learned the rules of the palace. So it was with Queen Esther. She dressed in beautiful gowns. She used delicious-smelling perfumes. And she learned the rules of her new home, the palace.

One important palace rule was: "Do not come to the king unless he calls you." If anyone, even the queen, displeased the king by breaking this rule, the person could be sentenced to death.

Perhaps this rule would not have mattered to Esther if it had not been for a royal official named Haman. Haman was a rich man and important. He was also very proud. When the king gave the command that people should bow and honor Haman, Haman expected everyone to do just that.

But Esther's cousin, Mordecai, would not bow down, and Haman became very, very angry! Soon Haman thought of a way to get rid of Mordecai. In fact, Haman planned to get rid of all of Mordecai's people.

Haman said to the king, "There is a certain group of people who live among us. They are different from us, and they do not obey our laws. Please issue a decree so that we may get rid of all these people."

Sadly, the king agreed to Haman's evil plan!

Now God's people were in terrible danger, for they were the ones Haman planned to destroy. When Esther heard of the plot, she was upset and afraid. No one in the palace knew Esther was one of God's people too.

Esther could not stand by and watch her people die. But what could she do? Esther asked all her friends to pray with her. She knew God could help her be brave.

Esther did not forget the palace rule: "Do not come to the king unless he calls you." But Esther had to speak to the king. She had to save her people. Esther decided to go against the palace rule.

"If I die, I die," Esther said. And she bravely walked into the king's throne room.

The king was pleased when he saw Esther standing before him. He extended his scepter to her. This was a sign that her life would be spared.

"What is your request?" asked the king.

"Grant me my life and spare my people," Esther said, "for our enemy Haman has a plot to destroy us all!"

When the king heard this, he immediately put an end to the evil plan against God's people, and Haman was punished for trying to trick the king.

Esther was made queen because of her beauty. But it was because of her courage that God's people were saved.

Let's Talk about It

1. Who was the king's favorite girl in the kingdom?

2. What did the king want everyone in the kingdom to do?

3. What did Haman want the king to do when Mordecai refused to bow down?

4. What could happen to Esther if she went to visit the king without being called?

5. What did Esther do that was brave?

Matching Items

king

bow down

queen

crown

Word Search

```
E  X  V  C  O  M  Z  T
H  V  T  O  J  O  H  H
P  Z  A  M  V  D  M  R
B  I  I  R  G  G  A  O
V  E  Y  T  B  N  S  N
O  V  Z  I  U  I  H  E
O  X  K  N  U  K  Z  E
M  E  L  P  O  E  P  I
```

Find these words

BRAVE • PEOPLE • THRONE • KINGDOM

Puzzle made at www.puzzlemaker.discoveryeducation.com.

Craft Activity

Make your own scepter!

Things you will need:

- paper towel tube (wrapping paper tubes make giant scepters!)
- markers or crayons
- decorative items like glitter, jewels, stickers, colored cereal loops
- glue
- aluminum foil

What to do:

1. Use the markers or crayons and other items to decorate your scepter.
2. Make it fancy by gluing on decorative items.
3. Crumple a large piece of aluminum foil into a large ball.
4. Squish the large ball into the end of the paper towel tube so it sticks out the end.
5. Wait for the glue to dry on your scepter and then play pretend!

COLORING PAGE

COLORING PAGE

Shape a lifestyle of faith expression in your child — Our passion is to provide a creative outlet for kids to

express their faith in a fun and meaningful way. Cultivate a deeper connection as you teach your child about the impact of God's love, building a legacy of relationship, creativity, and faith to last a lifetime.

Using interactive games, puzzles, and other activities, **Faith That Sticks resources** are a great go-to place for parents who want to teach their kids to love God and to know how much he loves them!

learn more at faiththatsticks.com

More about Reading Levels

PRE-READERS

Books appropriate for pre-readers have

- pictures that reinforce the text
- simple words
- short, simple sentences
- repetition of words and patterns
- large print

BEGINNING READERS

Books appropriate for beginning readers have

- pictures that reinforce the text
- intermediate words
- longer sentences
- simple stories
- dialogue between story characters

INDEPENDENT READERS

Books appropriate for independent readers have

- less need for pictorial support with the text
- more advanced vocabulary
- paragraphs
- longer stories
- more complex subjects

"There are perhaps no days of our childhood we lived so fully as those we spent with a favorite book." — MARCEL PROUST